Pebble® Plus

Habitats around the World

Life in a Pond

by Craig Hammersmith

CAPSTONE PRESS
a capstone imprint

Pebble Plus is published by Capstone Press,
1710 Roe Crest Drive, North Mankato, Minnesota 56003.
www.capstonepub.com

Library of Congress Cataloging-in-Publication Data
Hammersmith, Craig.
  Life in a pond / by Craig Hammersmith.
    p. cm. — (Pebble plus: Habitats around the world)
  Includes bibliographical references and index.
  Summary: "Color photos and simple text describe animals and their adaptations to a pond habitat"—Provided by
publisher.
  ISBN 978-1-4296-6816-3 (library binding)
  ISBN 978-1-4296-7149-1 (paperback)
  1. Pond animals—Adaptation—Juvenile literature. I. Title. II. Series.
  QL146.3.H357 2012
  591.763'6—dc22   2011005315

Editorial Credits
Gillia Olson, editor; Lori Bye, designer; Svetlana Zhurkin, media researcher; Laura Manthe, production specialist

Photo Credits
Alamy/blickwinkel, 13; F1online digitale Bildagentur, 5; Roderick Paul Walker, 10–11; Wildlife, 18–19
Shutterstock/blewisphotography, 20; Bull's-Eye Arts, 14–15; dan_nurgitz, 21; Daniel Hebert, 17; Durden Images, cover;
    Matt Hart, 9; pix2go, 1; William Attard McCarthy, 6–7

Note to Parents and Teachers

The Habitats around the World series supports national science standards related to life science.
This book describes and illustrates animals that live in ponds. The images support early readers
in understanding the text. The repetition of words and phrases helps early readers learn new
words. This book also introduces early readers to subject-specific vocabulary words, which are
defined in the Glossary section. Early readers may need assistance to read some words and to
use the Table of Contents, Glossary, Read More, Internet Sites, and Index sections of the book.

Printed and bound in the USA.
002247

Table of Contents

Pond Life

Plop! Splash! Kerplunk! Shallow ponds are smaller than lakes, but they are bursting with life. Ponds are home to all kinds of animals.

Insects

Insects live in calm pond waters.

Dragonflies lay eggs in ponds.

Young dragonflies live in water

until they become adults.

Frogs

Frogs live in and around ponds.
Young frogs, called tadpoles,
live underwater. Then they
grow legs and lungs. As adults,
they breathe outside of water.

Mud Puppies

Mud puppies live in ponds too.

Mud puppies aren't puppies.

They are amphibians like frogs
and salamanders.

11

Fish

Freshwater fish live in ponds.
Catfish, sunfish, and bass
can all be found in ponds.
They munch on insects and
plants in the water.

catfish

Turtles

Ponds are often home to turtles.
Turtles spend time swimming
in the water. But they also rest
in sunny places to warm up.

Birds

Birds go to ponds to find food.

Herons stand very still

in the shallow water.

When fish swim by, herons

spear them with their bills.

Beavers

Beavers don't just live in ponds. Sometimes they make ponds! They chew down trees to build dams. The dam blocks up the water and makes a new pond.

Fun Facts

~~~ Dragonflies can't fly when their wing muscles are cold.

~~~ In cold weather, fish can live under the pond's ice. They breathe air in the water that is trapped under the ice.

Beavers build dams to surround their home, or lodge, with water. The water keeps predators away.

Mud puppies are also called "mud puppies" and "water dogs." People once thought they barked like dogs!

Glossary

amphibian—a cold-blooded animal with a backbone and wet skin; frogs and mud puppies are amphibians

dam—a wall built to stop water from flowing in a stream or a river

insect—a small animal with a hard outer shell, six legs, three body sections, and two antennae; most insects have wings

lung—a body part that animals use to breathe

predator—an animal that hunts other animals for food

shallow—not deep

tadpole—a young frog; tadpoles hatch from eggs and live underwater

Read More

Animal Babies in Ponds and Rivers. Boston: Kingfisher, 2007.

Falwell, Cathryn. *Pond Babies.* Camden, Maine: Down East Books, 2011.

Worth, Bonnie. *Would You Rather Be a Pollywog?: All about Pond Life.* The Cat in the Hat's Learning Library. New York: Random House, 2010.

Internet Sites

FactHound offers a safe, fun way to find Internet sites related to this book. All of the sites on FactHound have been researched by our staff.

Here's all you do:

Visit *www.facthound.com*

Type in this code: 9781429668163

Index

Word Count: 183 (main text)
Grade: 1
Early-Intervention Level: 17